PICTURE LIBRARY

RACE CARS

PICTURE LIBRARY
RACE CARS

Norman Barrett

Franklin Watts

London   New York   Sydney   Toronto

First Paperback Edition 1990
ISBN 0-531-15175-1

© 1987 Franklin Watts

First published in Great Britain
   1987 by
Franklin Watts
12a Golden Square
London WIR 4BA

First published in the USA by
Franklin Watts Inc
387 Park Avenue South
New York
N.Y. 10016

First published in Australia by
Franklin Watts
14 Mars Road
Lane Cove
2066 NSW

UK ISBN: 0 86313 494 7
US ISBN: 0-531-10275-0
Library of Congress Catalog Card
Number 86-50641

Printed in Italy

Designed by
Barrett & Willard

Photographs by
Keith Barber
N.S. Barrett Collection
Dick Berggren
Steve Botham
Blay & McCormack
Graham Brown
F.G. Buss
Jim Crucefix
Daytona International Speedway
Ford Motor Company
Russell Hobman
John Hyam
Victor Lakey
E. Setchell
B. Watson

Illustration by
Rhoda & Robert Burns

Technical Consultant
Paul Huggett

Contents

Introduction

Motor racing takes many forms. To some people it means grand prix racing, on road circuits with sharp bends and turns in one-seater racing machines. But there are many other kinds of motor sport around the world.

Racing around oval circuits in all types of race cars is popular in both the United States and Europe. The sport is exciting as the cars hurtle round the track at high speed.

△ Stock car racing in the United States. This is the major US sport, especially in the South, where it takes place on huge oval tracks.

The big motor sport in the United States is stock car racing. High-speed, modified sedans race around big, steeply banked oval tracks.

Some of the classes that take part in oval racing in Europe are also called stock cars. Various classes of cars, some specially built, race on small oval tracks, sometimes on grass. In some classes, contact between cars is permitted. Oval racing is popular in Britain.

△ One type of stock car racing in Europe. These specially built Formula I stock cars race around small oval tracks. There is a lot of contact between the cars.

The story of race cars

Ford Thunderbird body shell covers a specially strong, purpose-built chassis and a powerful engine

Airfoil to help keep car on track at speed

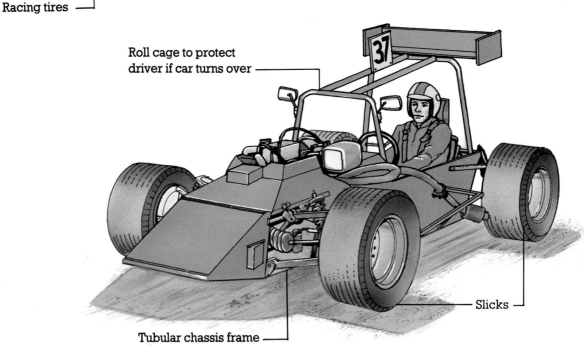

Racing tires

1 US Stock car

Roll cage to protect driver if car turns over

Slicks

Tubular chassis frame

2 Midget car

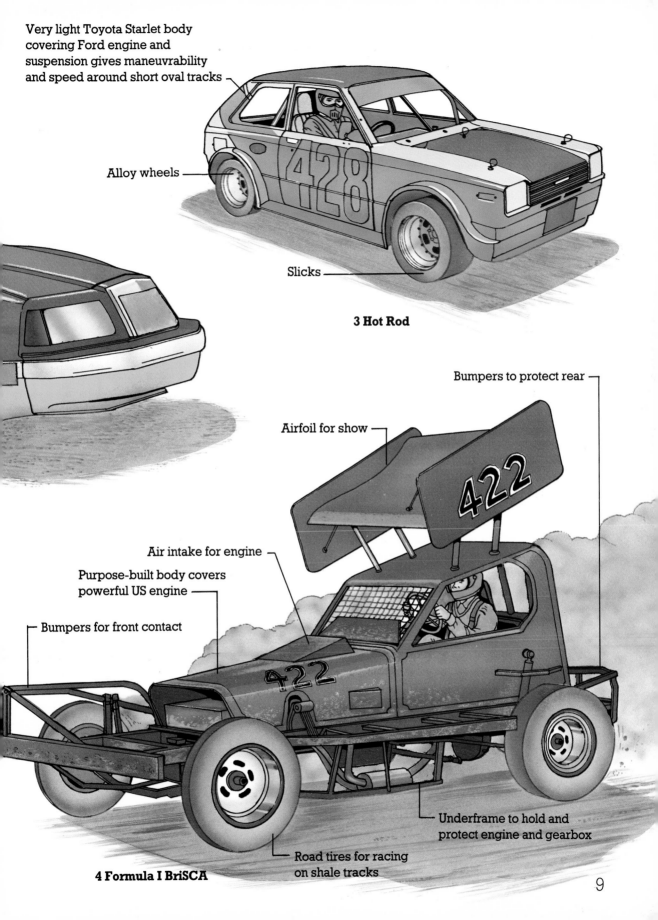

Very light Toyota Starlet body covering Ford engine and suspension gives maneuvrability and speed around short oval tracks

Alloy wheels

Slicks

3 Hot Rod

Bumpers to protect rear

Airfoil for show

Air intake for engine

Purpose-built body covers powerful US engine

Bumpers for front contact

Underframe to hold and protect engine and gearbox

Road tires for racing on shale tracks

4 Formula I BriSCA

Super speedways

Stock car racing in the United States is run under NASCAR rules. NASCAR stands for the National Association for Stock Car Auto Racing. Racing takes place mainly on the "super speedways" of the South. The most famous speedway is at Daytona, in Florida.

US stock cars are based on current midsize coupes and sedans. Vehicles such as sports cars, jeeps, station wagons and trucks are not used.

▷ Before and during a race, work is carried out on the car in the pits. Cars pull in at the pits for refueling, changes of tires and any repairs.

▽ A stock car race in progress at Daytona International Speedway. Strong safety netting protects the spectators in case of accidents. The drivers are also protected. They wear special safety equipment and the cars are reinforced.

▷ It looks like a traffic jam, but these powerful stock cars are traveling at high speed as they take a tight turn.

Tracks are banked to allow greater speeds when taking corners. A driver would have to take a bend much more slowly on a level track. Otherwise the car would tend to run straight off the track into the wall.

Stock cars are modified to produce high speeds, but they run on regular gasoline. Speeds vary according to the track. At North Wilkesboro, North Carolina, speeds of 250 mph (400 km/h) have been reached.

Drivers compete in a series of Grand National races ranging from 400 to 600 miles (644-966 km). The one who wins the most points during the year is the Grand National Champion.

△ Not all stock car racing in the United States is for big, powerful cars racing over 200 laps. This is a Sportsman class stock car in the pits at Darlington Raceway. The class is usually to be found on the shorter asphalt circuits.

14

Saloon car racing

The closest thing to US stock car racing in Europe is "saloon car" racing. But it takes place on big racing circuits, rather than high-speed ovals.

A "saloon car" is the British name for a production sedan. There are events for standard production models and for specially modified sedans. Races are divided into classes, according to engine size.

▽ Two small British Fords battle it out on the Brands Hatch racing circuit, in southern England. Modified saloon cars are designed for racing, with increased engine power, special gear ratios and wide racing tires.

Oval racing

Oval racing takes place on small circuits, up to about 400 m (¼mile) in Europe and 800–1600 m (½–1 mile) in the United States. As many as 20 cars might race over some 25 laps.

  Various types of cars are raced in separate classes. Racing is often organized locally or perhaps by a group of stadiums, so the names of the different classes can be confusing.

△ A Formula I stock car race in New Zealand. These are European-style stock cars.

▷ Formula I stock car racing in England. The driver of number 59 finds himself airborne as he runs out of room. These are BriSCA Formula I cars, the most powerful class on the European circuit. BriSCA stands for British Stock Car Association.

▽ The Super Modified, a popular class on the smaller oval raceways in the United States.

◁ A Superstox race, one of several classes run by the Spedeworth promoters in Britain.

▽ Spedeworth Formula I stock cars. These are smaller than the BriSCA Formula I cars.

Contact between cars is allowed in most of the open-wheel classes. But Midgets and US Super Modifieds are both non-contact classes.

Drivers earn points in races throughout the season. In some classes they are graded, and paint the color of their car roofs according to their grade.

There is little international oval-track racing, and "world championships" may often be local affairs.

▽ Hot Rods line up at the start. This is one of the most popular classes of stock car racing in Europe. Intentional contact between cars is not allowed, so passing on the tight oval track requires great skill.

◁ Hot Rods battling for the lead on a bend. These medium-sized lightweight sedans provide exciting racing. In Britain, the National Hot Rod Promoters Association stages a world title event.

▽ Super Rods are larger versions of Hot Rods, with more powerful engines.

▷ Stock Rods are a smaller and cheaper version of the Hot Rods. They have smaller engines and road-going tires. As with Hot Rods, intentional contact is not permitted. But the car in the middle of the three Stock Rods locked in combat does not have any say in the matter!

▽ A Dirt Modified, a US class of car that runs on the small dirt tracks.

A race is for cars of one class only. Several classes are included in some race meetings. Other meetings might be devoted to just one class, such as Hot Rods or Formula I stock cars.

Some oval racing fans enjoy watching all types of racing. But others faithfully follow their own favorite class of cars, with its familiar drivers and models.

▽ Stock Saloons are heavily reinforced. Contact is not only allowed, it is expected. The class provides some of the toughest motor sport in the world. The cars are so strong that they rarely finish up as wrecks.

△ Strictly speaking, there is only one way around the track, but these Stock Saloons appear to be traveling in opposite directions.

▷ "Bangers is a British "race 'em and wreck 'em" class. Almost any kind of production sedan can take part, although no engine modifications are allowed. There are strict safety precautions, but many a car ends up as a complete wreck.

Autograss

Autograss is a form of oval racing particularly popular in England and Wales. The circuits are laid out specially for meetings, usually in a flat field rented from a farmer or other landowner.

There are classes for production sedans based on engine size, and for Specials. These are cars specially built for high-speed racing on grass and dirt.

△ Autograss Specials are fast open-wheeled cars. They have engines mounted behind the driver to put more weight on the rear wheels. This gives the tires more grip on dirt tracks.

The weather plays a big part in autograss racing as it affects the condition of the track. Racing on muddy or dusty tracks calls for different driving skills.

The cars are strongly built. They are fitted with the kind of tires that give plenty of grip on loose surfaces.

National championships are held for both men and women, and there is a Junior class for drivers aged 14 to 17 years.

▽ A Class 7 Saloon, one of the most powerful of the autograss Sedan classes.

Midget cars

Midget race cars are specially constructed small cars with a light but strong chassis and an open cockpit. They are among the fastest cars on the oval raceways.

In Europe, Midgets are mostly rear-engined. In the United States they are more like smaller versions of the Sprint cars.

▽ A Midget is something like a racing car in miniature. The airfoil and wide rear tires, called "slicks," provide a firm grip on the track for high-speed racing.

Ministox

In Britain there is a special class, called Ministox, for drivers between the ages of 10 and 16. It serves as a starter class for future oval racers, and both boys and girls compete.

The cars are standard small-engined Minis, small British economy cars, with special reinforcements. Contact is permitted, but there are strict safety precautions and drivers wear protective clothing.

△ A young Ministox driver sits proudly on the hood of his car. For racing, he will wear a helmet and other safety equipment, and the car is reinforced all around.

The story of race cars

How motor sport began

The automobile was invented over a hundred years ago, and it was not long before the owners of the first vehicles began to race each other on the public roads. As the sport began to be organized, special cars were developed for racing and special circuits were built. Motor racing became a worldwide sport.

△ Early motor races took place on public roads.

Branching out

Motor sport branched out in several directions. The most international branch of motor racing is grand prix racing, and there are major events for sports cars, too. The race cars described in this book compete in oval racing, which developed in different ways.

US stock car racing

In the United States, stock car racing began in the 1930s as a cheap form of motor racing. As many as 100 modified old cars would provide spectacular racing on a dirt track or a beach.

But the sport changed its form in 1947, when NASCAR was founded. Pepped-up production-line sedans racing at high speed around steeply banked ovals captured the public imagination. Stock car racing is now the major motor sport in the United States.

△ Stock car racing became the major motor sport in the United States.

Rough and tumble

Stock car racing in Britain began as a rough and tumble sport. There had been some Midget racing in the 1940s, but the first stock car meeting took place in 1954, inspired by the short-track racing seen in the United States and France. It was held on the tight 280 yd (256 m) oval at New Cross, in London. Contact between cars was allowed. The crowd enjoyed this new "race 'em and wreck 'em" type of sport, and it caught on.

△ A Midget car of the late 1940s.

A "circus"

The stock car craze in Britain lasted for about two years. But, because of the intentional contacts, "real" motor racing enthusiasts regarded stock car racing as a "circus," and fewer people came to watch it.

The crowds come back

A few promoters, however, continued to stage stock car events. New classes and different types of car were developed and raced by rival promoters. As a result, stock car racing did not grow as a national sport in Britain.

Gradually, the crowds came back. Racing on the small oval circuits was packed with excitement, and the fans could see what was happening all the time. The sport spread to other parts of Europe and to countries as far afield as South Africa and New Zealand.

Classes such as the BriSCA Formula I and the Spedeworth Hot Rods became major attractions. Even the "race 'em and wreck 'em" style returned, with the introduction of the Banger class.

△ A typical stock car racing incident in Britain in the 1960s.

△ Stock car racing in New Zealand.

Facts and records

Daytona International Speedway

The super speedways are enormous tracks. Daytona has a 2.5 miles (4 km) D-shaped track, which is 40 ft (12 m) wide. At places, the banking is more than 30 degrees. Tremendous speeds can be reached on the 3,000 ft (915 m) back straightway. The grandstands seat 75,000 spectators, and there is infield parking for 25,000 cars.

△ Speeding along a straightway at Daytona International Speedway.

King Richard

The undisputed "king" of US stock car racing is Richard Petty. He was Grand National Champion seven times, between 1964 and 1979, and won the Daytona 500 seven times (1964–81). His father, Lee Petty, was Grand National Champion twice, and won the first Daytona 500 in 1959.

World Championships

There are numerous World Championships for European stock car racing, held mainly in Britain. They include world titles for BriSCA Formulas I and II, Spedeworth Superstox and Hot Rods and even Bangers.

△ A world champion in action— unlikely as this might seem. Jan Scott of Czechoslovakia won the first Superstox World Championship in 1961.

Glossary

Autograss
A British form of oval racing held on temporary flat grass or dirt tracks.

Banger
A British class for old sedans in which contact often happens.

Banking
Parts of the track that slope up to the outside, enabling the cars to go faster around turns.

Formula I stock cars
Open-wheel classes of car in Europe. There are two different Formula I classes, staged by rival organizations.

Hot Rods
A European class for modified production cars. The racing on small European tracks looks like US stock car racing in miniature.

Midgets
Very small open-wheeled cars.

Ministox
A British class for young drivers, 10–16 years old.

Modified
A car that has been adapted for racing.

Oval Racing
Another name for European stock car racing.

Special
A car specially built for racing.

Sprint car
A special built for short track racing in the United States.

Stock car racing
In the United States this is mainly high speed racing of modified sedans on super speedways. In Europe, it is contact racing on small oval circuits.

Stock Rods
Cheaper versions of the Hot Rods with less powerful engines.

Stock Saloons
Heavily reinforced sedans that knock each other about as they around the track.

Super Rods
Larger versions of the Hot Rods.

Super speedways
The great US oval tracks.

Superstox
A class of open-wheeled specials for contact racing.

Index